Big Machines

TRACTORS

By Katie Kawa

 Gareth Stevens
Publishing

Please visit our website, www.garethstevens.com. For a free color catalog of all our high-quality books, call toll free 1-800-542-2595 or fax 1-877-542-2596.

Library of Congress Cataloging-in-Publication Data

Kawa, Katie.
Tractors / Katie Kawa.
    p. cm. — (Big machines)
Includes index.
ISBN 978-1-4339-5572-3 (pbk.)
ISBN 978-1-4339-5573-0 (6-pack)
ISBN 978-1-4339-5570-9 (library binding)
1. Tractors—Juvenile literature. I. Title.
TL233.15.K39 2012
629.225'2—dc22

2011006572

First Edition

Published in 2012 by
Gareth Stevens Publishing
111 East 14th Street, Suite 349
New York, NY 10003

Copyright © 2012 Gareth Stevens Publishing

Editor: Katie Kawa
Designer: Daniel Hosek

Photo credits: Cover and all interior images Shutterstock.com.

Printed in the United States of America

CPSIA compliance information: Batch #CS11GS: For further information contact Gareth Stevens, New York, New York at 1-800-542-2595.

Contents

Tractors are used
on farms.

They pull tools that
help farmers.

Tractors pull heavy things. This is why they are slow.

Tractors use many tools.
One tool is a plow.

A plow has teeth. The teeth dig up dirt.

Tractors get dirt ready for seeds. Plants come from the seeds!

Some tractors cut grass. These are garden tractors.

Tractors have four wheels. They move well in dirt.

Two wheels are big.
Two wheels are small.

A tractor pull is
a game. Strong
tractors win!

Words to Know

plow   teeth   wheels

Index